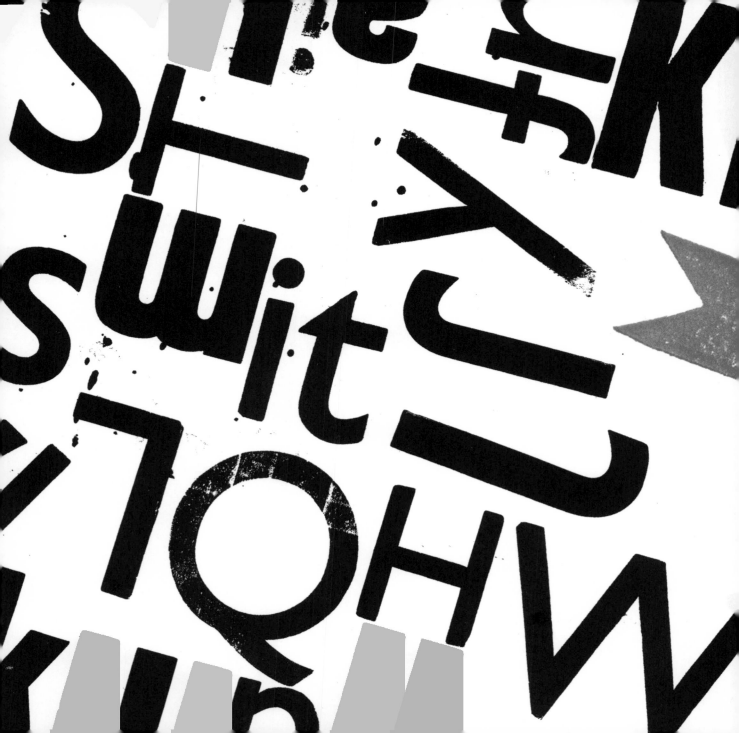

Printer's ABC

Diana Dăgădiță

Published 2019
by Design For Today

A

is for Adana, Ampersand, Ascenders

is for Brayer, Borders, Blocks

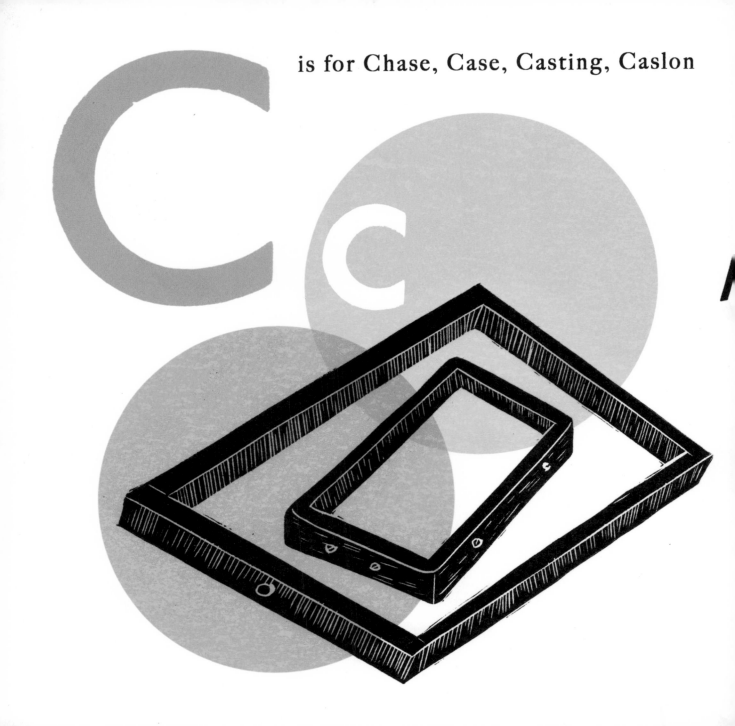

is for Chase, Case, Casting, Caslon

E is for Ems & Ens, Elrod, Expanded, Elephant

F is for Furniture, Fleurons, Fount, Flong

is for Gloves, Glint, Galley, Gutenberg

H h is for Hell box, Hot metal, Heidelberg

is for Ink, Imposing stone, Impression

Jj
is for Jobbing stick, Jigger, Justification

is for Key, Koenig, Kerning, Knife

is for Ludlow, Linotype, Ligature, Leading

M m

is for Manicule, Make ready, Monotype

N n

is for Nuts and bolts, Nick, Nonpareil

is for Oil, Old cut, Octavo, Overtime

is for Pilcrow, Pica, Pi, Proof, Point

Q is for Quoins, Quads, Quotes

R r

is for Registration, Reglet, Recto

S is for Slug cutter, Specimen, Script, Sorts

Tt

is for Typescale, Token, Tracing paper

U u

is for Unlock, Uppercase, Universal

is for Vandercook, Viscosity, Verona

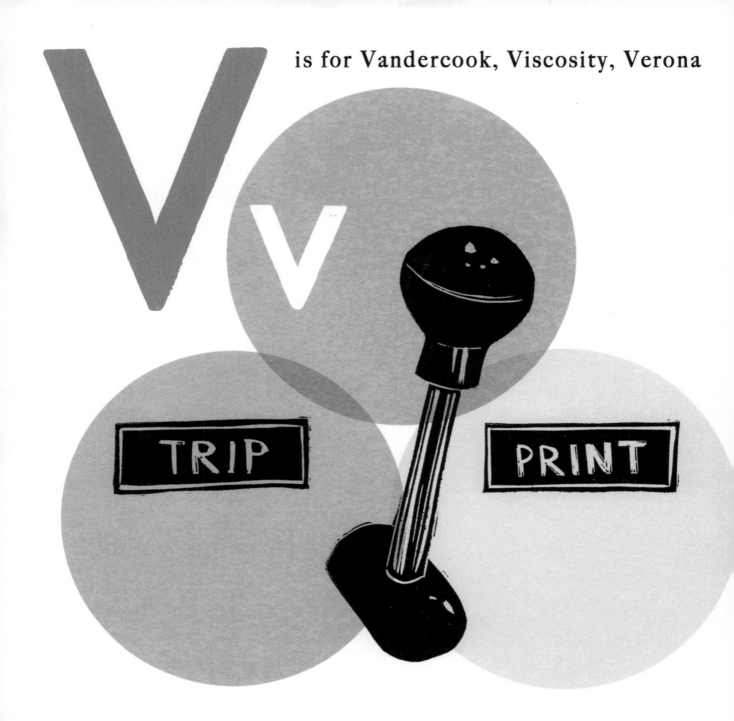

is for Whip, Whack, Waffle,

is for Youthline

& Z is for Zapf and Zincos.

goose

ipt,

X is for Xylography, Xylonite, X-height,

Adana
Printing presses manufactured by Adana 1922-1999, best known for their "Eight-Five" hand platen press (*illustrated*).

Ampersand
& - The abbreviation or sign for the word "and", originated as a ligature of the letters "et" (*lat.*)

Ascenders
The part of a letter that extends above the level of the x-height (eg. b, d, f, h, k, t) (see x-height)

Block
A general term used for woodcuts, electros, or zincos from which an impression is taken.

Border
A printed decorative strip around the edge of a sheet of paper (see fleurons)

Brayer
Roller; a hand-tool used in printing and printmaking to spread a thin, even layer of ink.

Case
Type case; the receptacle in which type is laid to compose from. When in pairs, they're defined as upper and lower, respectively. Traditionally, the capital letters were stored in a separate drawer, or case, placed above the case holding the other letters (this is why the capital letters are called "uppercase" characters, and the minuscules are "lower case").

Caslon
The name given to serif typefaces designed by William Caslon I (c. 1692–1766), or inspired by his work.

Casting
Type casting; a technique for casting the individual letters known as sorts used in hot metal typesetting by pouring molten metal into brass moulds called matrices.

Chase
An iron frame, cast or wrought, to hold the type for printing.

Devil
Printer's; an apprentice in a printing establishment who performed tasks, such as mixing inks, fetching and dissing type, cleaning equipment, and who often ended up covered in black ink.

Dirty proof
A proof-sheet that contains many uncorrected errors, or proofing and other marks.

Dissing
Distributing the type back into the case after a printing job. From "dis", abbreviation of the word "distribute".

Elephant
A size of printing paper (30 x 23 inches), writing or drawing paper (28 x 23 inches), brown paper (34 x 24 inches).

Elrod

A caster created by Benjamin Elrod in 1917. The machine is an extrusion-type device with type metal entering the mould on one side and then cooling, solidifying and being pulled from the mould on the other. The Elrod Press, run by Andy Taylor, has one of the few remaining Elrods in use.

Em

An em is a spacing size, traditionally the width of the capital "M" on a metal character block. *(Mutton)*

En

An en is a typographic unit, half of the width of an em, traditionally the size of the uppercase 'N'. *(Nut)*

Expanded

A font in which the set widths of the characters are wider than in the standard typeface; the reverse of condensed.

Fleurons

Flowers; ornaments used to make borders for cards, pages, and wrappers, and for embellishing chapter headings, or forming tail-pieces to books.

Flong

A material, usually pulped paper or cardboard, used for making moulds in stereotyping.

Fount

The term applied to the number of letters constituting a complete fount of any particular class of face or body.

Furniture

The wooden, metal, resin-composite or even resalite blocks that surround the type or plate base to hold it in place.

Galley

A long, narrow tray, usually of metal, for holding type that has been set.

Glint

Ornamental metal type (B1309 and B1310), loved and used extensively especially by members of the 'Glint Club' and players of the 'Glint Game'.

Gloves

Essential hand covering for all printers, especially when cleaning up.

Gutenberg

Johannes; (c 1400 – 1468) German blacksmith, goldsmith, inventor, printer, and publisher. His introduction of mechanical movable type printing to Europe in 1439 started the Printing Revolution.

Heidelberg

The Original Heidelberg Platen Press was a letterpress printing press manufactured by the Heidelberger Druckmaschinen company in Germany. It was often referred to as the "Windmill", after the shape and movement of its paper feed system.

Hell box

A container for battered, unidentifiable, or broken sorts to be melted down and re-cast. In olden times a boot was used.

Hot metal

A typesetting technique in which type is newly made each time from molten metal, cast by a composing machine (see Linotype).

Imposing stone

A perfectly smooth stone or iron surface on which formes are imposed and corrected.

Impression

The pressure necessary to transfer a printed image from a printing plate, blanket, or other image carrier to the paper or other substrate. The term impression is also used to refer to a printed image.

Ink

The pigment of various colours which imparts the print to a sheet on impression being applied to type.

Jigger

A small box with divisions to hold peculiar sorts, usually made of quadrats and leads.

Jobbing stick

Composing stick; hand-held tool that type is set into, with lever attachment to aid the changing of measures.

Justification

Term applied generally to the even and equal spacing of words and lines to a given measure.

Kerning

The spacing between letters or characters in a piece of text to be printed.

Key

Quoin; a T-shaped metal tool used to lock/unlock the quoins (see quoins).

Knife

Palette; a blunt tool with a flexible steel blade, used for mixing or applying ink.

Koenig

Machine; a high-speed steam-powered printing press designed by German inventor Friedrich Koenig (17 April 1774 – 17 January 1833). This new style of printing press could print up to 1,100 sheets/hour, printing on both sides of the paper at the same time.

Leading

Lead strips of various widths and lengths used for spacing in between lines of type.

Ligature

Two or more letters cast in one piece, such as æ, ct, fl, Qu, Th, etc...

Linotype

Line-casting machine that produces an entire line of metal type at once, hence a line-o'-type - known as hot metal typesetting, it was a significant improvement over the previous industry practice of hand-setting letter by letter.

Ludlow

(*illustrated, a Ludlow matrix cabinet*) A Ludlow Typograph is a hot metal typesetting system. The device casts slugs of type which are used for the actual printing, and then melted down and recycled on the spot.

Makeready

Set up; The process of setting up and adjusting a printing press for a particular ink, paper and specifications prior to printing. This includes matching the printed piece with the proof to be sure everything is correct.

Manicule

Symbol in the shape of a pointing hand, used to draw attention to a section of text. The symbol originates in scribal tradition of the medieval and Renaissance period, appearing in the margin of manuscripts to mark corrections or notes.

Monotype

A mechanized typecasting device that enabled a keyboard operator to set type by punching holes in a paper ribbon, which then triggered the casting of individual letters.

Nick

The groove or grooves placed in the shank of a letter to assist composition, and to discriminate between different founts. Also any scratch, hole, or other such imperfection in a blade or other surface.

Nonpareil

In metal typography, a term for a slug of type six points thick. Half of a pica in depth of body;

Nuts & Bolts

Every printer needs a set of reliable spanners! In typography, a nut is a slang term for an en space.

Oil

The viscous liquid that keeps the presses turning, the rust away, and the printer happy.

Octavo

A printed sheet that has been folded three times to yield eight leaves or sixteen pages. Abbreviated 8vo and 8°.

Old cut

Founts similar to the Caslon old-faced type, and others related to those used in Venice in the fifteenth century.

Overtime

Late or night work that involves an extra charge on labour.

Pica

Typesetting unit of measurement commonly used for measuring lines of type. One pica equals 12 points, and there are 6 picas to an inch (actually, 6 picas equal 0.996 inch).

Pi

Broken or indiscriminately mixed type. Less than appetising printer's pi calls forth unprintable language.

Pilcrow

The pilcrow (¶) can be used as an indent for separate paragraphs or to designate a new paragraph in one long piece of copy. The pilcrow was a type of rubrication used in the Middle Ages to mark a new train of thought, before discrete paragraphs were commonplace. ¶

Point

The point is the basic unit of measurement used in typography. A point size is roughly 1/72nd of an inch.

Proof

A trial print of any forme of type, plates, or blocks.

Quads
Short for the word "quadrat", a metal spacer used in letterpress typesetting.

Quoins
In handset typography, a wooden or metal wedge used to secure type in the frame after hand tightening.

Quotes
The upturned commas (" & ") and apostrophes (' & ') used respectively for identifying quoted matter.

Recto
The odd-numbered right-hand pages of any work, from the Latin phrase recto folio, meaning "on the right-hand leaf.".

Registration
The arrangement of two or more printed images in exact alignment with each other.

Reglet
A thin strip of wood or metal used as furniture (see furniture) in locking up (securing the metal type in a frame).

Script
Sloping type similar in character to handwriting. In script typefaces, letters are connected.

Slug Cutter
A device used for cutting slugs (blank strips of lead made by an Elrod machine) which are used as spacing between lines of type.

Sorts
The general term applied to any particular letter or letters as distinguished from a complete fount.

Specimen
Type specimen book; printed brochures or catalogues of type foundries and printers, advertising the range and quality of type available.

Token
Two hundred and fifty impressions are reckoned as such.

Tracing Paper
Another essential piece of printer's equipment, used to check layouts and positioning of type.

Type scale
Rules used for measurement in points and picas.

Universal
Machine; A jobbing platen machine for steam or treadle, manufactured by Messrs. Hopkinson and Cope.

Unlock
To unfasten a forme, allegedly previously with mallet and shooting stick, but today with a quoin key.

Uppercase
The term comes from how printers organized their type cabinets. The capital letters, which were used less often, were kept in higher cases, hence the name "uppercase" (also see case)

Vandercook
The proofing press, manufactured by Vandercook and Sons, the first press to use a geared cylinder, thus easier and more precise for the operator to use.
Verona
Typeface credited to Robert Wiebking, 1924, named after the Italian city, Verona, still a centre of printing.
Viscosity
The property of a fluid, such as a printing ink, that describes the degree of its resistance to flow, or its ability to adhere to a surface.

Waffle
A slang term sometimes used by printers, meaning twaddle, gossip, or jaw. Waffling is also the term used to describe a printing and paper defect caused by the mechanical stress of thick offset printing ink.
Whack!
An exclamation of disbelief much used by printers.
Whip
A slang term for a more than ordinarily quick compositor.

X-height
In typography, the height of the lowercase letter "x," A character's x-height does not take into account ascenders or descenders and is thus a more realistic measurement of the size of a typeface than point size. Also known as body height and body size.
Xylography
The art of engraving on wood or of printing from woodblocks.
Xylonite
A durable synthetic material used in the construction of tint blocks which are used to put down large blocks of colour.

Youthline script
Hugely popular script type designed by Stephenson Blake in 1952. An ad from "Typographica' No.6 reads: 'The name of this new script type is Youthline: it has several interesting features, and one that is quite unique in a script type: it has virtually no kerning overhangs.'

Zapf
Hermann (November 8 1918 - June 4, 2015) calligrapher, type designer, and typographer who has designed more than 200 typefaces, many of which have become a part of our everyday experiences (Optima, Palatino, Zapfino, etc.).
Zincos
A short term for the zincograph process (a planographic process using zinc plates instead of the traditional limestones in lithography). It has also become a shorthand term for any line block.

PRINTER'S ABC

Diana Dăgădiţă's *Printer's ABC* was inspired by a visit to Andy Taylor's printing workshop in East Sussex. The original book was created as part of Diana's final major project of the BA Illustration course at Solent University and is an illustrated collection of tools and terms used by letterpress printers, then and now.

The capital letters were printed using found wooden type at the Solent Printroom and then scanned, as were the linocut illustrations.

The headings have been set in 16pt Old Caslon and the glossary in 10pt Old Caslon. The majority of the found wooden type used in the book is Gill Sans.

This edition first published in 2019 by Design For Today
88 Emmanuel Road, London, SW 12 0HR
www.designfortoday.co.uk

Illustrations © Diana Dăgădiţă
www.ephemre.com

ISBN: 978-1-912066-57-5

This book has been printed using offset lithography at
Graphius, Ghent in Belgium, on 150 gsm Arcoprint Milk White

DESIGN FOR TODAY
ephemera, objects of curiosity, books to read and touch

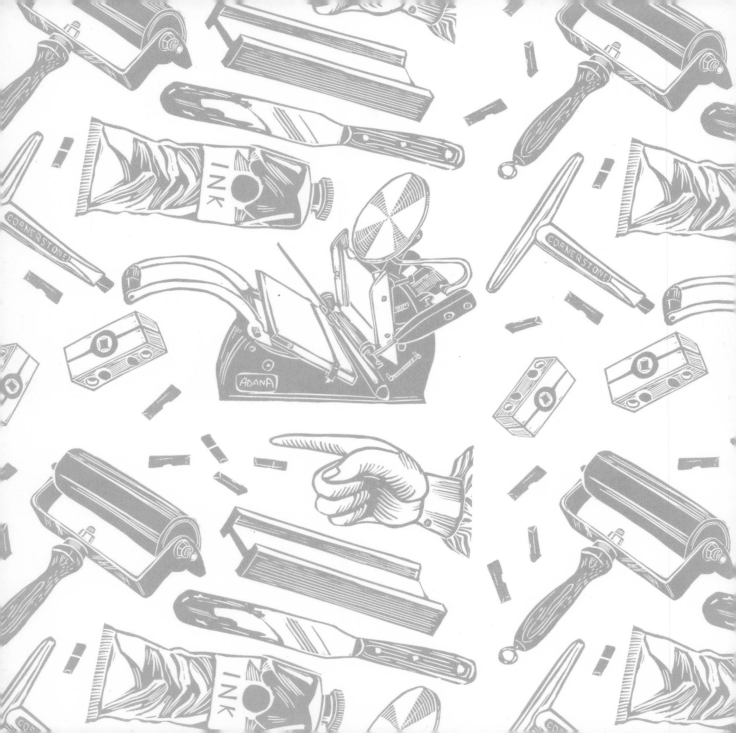